TULLY FILMUS

I. GLADYS. 1939. 30 X 24. COLLECTION DR. AND MRS. NORMAN AVNET.

TULLY FILMUS

INTRODUCTION BY ALFRED WERNER

CLEVELAND AND NEW YORK

THE WORLD PUBLISHING COMPANY

PUBLISHED BY THE WORLD PUBLISHING COMPANY
2231 WEST 110TH STREET, CLEVELAND 2, OHIO
PUBLISHED SIMULTANEOUSLY IN CANADA
BY NELSON, FOSTER & SCOTT LTD.
LIBRARY OF CONGRESS CATALOG CARD NUMBER: 63-18587
ALL RIGHTS RESERVED. NO PART OF THIS BOOK MAY BE REPRODUCED
IN ANY FORM WITHOUT WRITTEN PERMISSION FROM THE PUBLISHER, EXCEPT
FOR BRIEF PASSAGES INCLUDED IN A REVIEW APPEARING IN A NEWSPAPER OR
MAGAZINE. PRODUCED BY SHELLEY GRAPHICS, LTD., NEW YORK.
OFFSET PLATES AND ALL PRESSWORK BY INDUSTRIE GRAFICHE TOSO, TURIN.
PHOTO-ENGRAVINGS BY OFFICINE CROMOGRAFICHE BIANCHI E TENCONI, MILAN.
DESIGNED BY ABE LERNER. PRINTED IN ITALY.

Contents

A COMPREHENSIVE LIST OF PAINTINGS
BY TULLY FILMUS FOLLOWS
THE PLATES

LIST OF PLATES

22. Resting. 1945. 16 x 13. Collection of the artist.

23. Sketch Class. 1947. 24 x 14. ACA Gallery, New York.

24. The Sculptor. 1950. 32 x 16. ACA Gallery, New York.

25. Girl in the Mirror. 1951. 10 x 12. Collection Mr. and Mrs. Gerald Light, Kings Point, N.Y.

26. Alice. 1952. 16 x 12. ACA Gallery, New York.

27. Violinist. 1950. 18 x 28. Collection Mr. and Mrs. Lester Avnet, Kings Point, N.Y.

28. Demonstration. 1945. 52 x 30. Collection Mr. and Mrs. Lester Avnet, Kings Point, N.Y.

29. Flowered Hat. 1953. 14 x 11. Collection Mr. and Mrs. David Nelson, Woodmere, N.Y.

30. The Red Sweater. 1954. 14 x 11. Collection Gladys Filmus.

31. Two Girls. 1954. 17 x 13. Collection Mr. and Mrs. Reuben L. Kershaw, Great Neck, N.Y.

32. Dressing. 1954. 13 x 22. Collection Dr. and Mrs. Eugene Saland, Old Westbury, N.Y.

33. At the Museum. 1954. 30 x 16. ACA Gallery, New York.

34. The Flute Player. 1956. 11 x 14. Collection Dr. and Mrs. Arthur S. Carlson, Glen Cove, N.Y.

35. Music Makers. 1955. 20 x 26. Collection Mr. and Mrs. Arnold Rosenberg, Great Neck, N.Y.

36. Gossips. 1956. 16 x 20. ACA Gallery, New York.

37. Girl on Chair. 1954. 10 x 8. Collection Gladys Filmus.

38. Girl Reading. 1957. 14 x 11. ACA Gallery, New York.

39. April. 1955. 14 x 30. Collection Mr. and Mrs. Joseph Resnick, Ellenville, N.Y.

40. Rain. 1956. 22 x 12. Collection Dr. and Mrs. Sidney Samis, Kings Point, N.Y.

41. Exhibition Opening. 1957. 20 x 26. Collection Dr. and Mrs. Norman Avnet, Great Neck, N.Y.

42. Sunday in the Museum. 1957. 16 x 30. Collection Mr. and Mrs. Arthur P. Gould, Great Neck, N.Y.

43. Girl in Blue. 1958. 30 x 14. Collection Charles Avnet, Long Beach, N.Y.

44. Three Girls. 1957. 10 x 8. Collection Mr. and Mrs. Al Schwartz, Kings Point, N.Y.

45. At the Gallery. 1958. 16 x 20. Collection Mr. and Mrs. Seymour Kleinman, Great Neck, N.Y.

46. Nora. 1958. 34 x 23. ACA Gallery, New York.

47. Stooped Old Man. 1959. 24 x 14. ACA Gallery, New York.

48. Summer Rain. 1958. 13 x 24. Collection Mr. and Mrs. Martin C. Barell, Kings Point, N.Y.

49. Clown. 1957. 14 x 11. Collection Jonathan Avnet, Kings Point, N.Y.

50. Artist's Wife. 1960. 24 x 14. Collection of the artist.

51. Lisa. 1959. 34 x 20. Collection Mr. and Mrs. Lester Avnet, Kings Point, N.Y.

52. Pretzel Vendor. 1959. 14 x 11. Collection Chaim Shursha, Tel-Aviv, Israel.

53. Woman on Balcony. 1959. 30 x 16. Collection Mr. and Mrs. Sam Marks, Burbank, Calif.

54. Giovanna. 1960. 14 x 11. ACA Gallery, New York.

55. Circus Girl. 1963. 30 x 20. ACA Gallery, New York.

56. Backstage. 1958. 30 x 40. Collection Mr. and Mrs. Lester Avnet, Kings Point, N.Y.

57. Dressing Room. 1960. 26 x 36. Collection Mr. and Mrs. Lester Avnet, Kings Point, N.Y.

58. The Hora. 1958. 34 x 23. Collection Dr. and Mrs. Jack Rosen, Brooklyn, N.Y.

59. Reading Room. 1959. 20 x 30. ACA Gallery, New York.

60. Nude. 1959. 34 x 12. ACA Gallery, New York.

61. After Work. 1959. 26 x 10. ACA Gallery, New York.

62. Old Friends. 1960. 20 x 14. Collection Mr. and Mrs. Boris M. Tarna, Tokyo, Japan.

63. Morning Paper. 1960. ACA Gallery, New York.

64. The Discussion. 1962. 29 x 14. Collection Dr. and Mrs. Norman Avnet, Great Neck, N.Y.

65. Chassidic Dance. 1961. 36 x 28. Collection Dr. and Mrs. Norman Avnet, Great Neck, N.Y.

66. Point of Information. 1961. 16 x 30. ACA Gallery, New York.

67. Patriarch. 1961. 26 x 10. Collection Dr. and Mrs. Norman Avnet, Great Neck, N.Y.

68. Michael. 1962. 20 x 14. Collection Michael Roy Filmus.

69. Stephen. 1961. 20 x 14. Collection Stephen Isaac Filmus.

70. The Return. 1962. 26 x 12. ACA Gallery, New York.

71. Preserving the Torah. 1962. 23 x 34. ACA Gallery, New York.

72. Chamber Music. 1962. 36 x 26. ACA Gallery, New York.

73. Trio. 1962. 30 x 40. ACA Gallery, New York.

74. The Klezmer. 1961. 26 x 32. Collection Mr. and Mrs. Lester Avnet, Kings Point, N.Y.

75. The Orchestra. 1962. 30 x 40. Collection Mr. and Mrs. Lester Avnet, Kings Point, N.Y.

76. At the Piano. 1962. 14 x 19. Collection Mr. and Mrs. Lester Avnet, Kings Point, N.Y.

77. Print Collector. 1962. 24 x 20. Collection Dr. and Mrs. Theodore Robertson, Locust Valley, N.Y.

78. Connoisseur. 1961. 13 x 6. Collection of the artist.

79. The Concert. 1961. 30 x 40. Collection Mr. and Mrs. Robert H. Avnet, Los Angeles, Calif.

80. The Village. 1963. 30 x 50. ACA Gallery, New York.

81. Old Scholar. 1963. 10 x 8. Collection of the artist.

2. HORSE AND WAGON. 1940. 26 x 36. COLLECTION MR. AND MRS. LESTER AVNET.

The Painter Tully Filmus

BY ALFRED WERNER

THE painter Tully Filmus belongs in the proud tradition of American Realism that started in the 18th century with the first itinerant painters of New England. The term "realism" had not yet been coined. It was first used as an aesthetic term in the 1850s by a friend of the great French painter Courbet. This friend was a minor novelist named Champfleury, who in fact disliked labels and even considered the word *réalisme* a joke:

"Courbet alone has made use of it with the robust faith he is fortunate enough to possess and which makes it impossible for him to doubt. For a long time my sincerity made me hesitate to use the label, for I do not believe in it. Realism is as old as the world, and there have been realists in all ages...."

One does not have to be a prophet to add that there will be realists in all ages to come. In Courbet's time *réalisme* was as much a battle cry as New Realism is today. In neither is competition with photography intended or desired. When another of Courbet's friends, the poet Baudelaire, wrote of the "real painter" who would "know how to wrest from actual life its *epic quality* and make us see and understand how *great* and *poetic* we are in our neckties and polished shoes," he expressed, in the words I have italicized, the attributes that distinguish good art from bad, whether representational or nonrepresentational. And all good realist art is epic, great, poetic, whether produced in France by Courbet, in Germany by Liebermann, or in the U.S.A. by Eakins.

Art is born whenever man succeeds in transfiguring nature. To exalt, to glorify life, the artist has first of all to comprehend it. To be an artist, man trains himself in perception, to observe and understand the subtle relationships between masses, lines, and colors in nature, just as a musician trains himself to analyze the intricacies of polyphonic sound.

He develops the inner eye to comprehend the *Gestalt* behind and beneath a maze of apparently conflicting details, the hand with which to orchestrate the rhythms and a-rhythms, the harmonies and discordancies that define the shape of a man, a landscape, a flower. A genuine artist like Filmus is bound to blend the reporter's task of objectively recording appearances with the poet's privilege of imprinting subjective reaction upon external reality. Although obsessed with reality, he none the less scrutinizes each particle, cuts away the excrescences, and leaves it refined by mental processes exactly where it was, or where it should have been in the first place.

While calling him a realist, I must point out that, true artist that he is, he always infuses his own personality into the living flesh of an existence that cannot be transported like a parcel, but can be felt and resuscitated in feeling. He would not be worth talking about were he not more concerned with the expression of his inner world of feeling and imagination than with a slavish imitation of the world of appearances. For him, nature is only the spark igniting the flame of his desire to create. For him, neither perceiving nor fixing an image is ever a purely automatic result of skill, for the heart is the central agency co-ordinating the nerves of the fingers with those of the retina. Thus, Filmus goes beyond the subjection of nature to a stern formal analysis. In brief, beginning with observed reality, he paints as far as his *élan vital* can carry him away from precise reference to any objects in nature, and so provides the unity of form lacking in nature and transfigures, transubstantiates, reality.

All of this must be said in the preface to a book introducing the *oeuvre* of a man who, while he can hardly be called a neophyte—he has been a professional painter for more than thirty years—is not so widely known to the America of the 1960s as he should be. Filmus has received several much coveted awards, and he has exhibited in many American museums, some of which have acquired his works. Yet in the last few years he has participated in no group shows, nor has he taken the trouble to prepare one-man shows in an age in which it is assumed that a good artist who does not demonstrate his output annually must be dead. Apart from his colleagues and close friends, and apart from a few astute and discriminating collectors, he was known for years chiefly as a conscientious teacher of his craft, guiding with patience and a sense of responsibility the first steps of those who entrusted themselves to his knowledge and experience. The exhibition in October 1963 at the ACA Gallery, New York, was, surprisingly, his first comprehensive one-man show in more than twenty years.

It is easy to guess why he withdrew temporarily from the hustle and bustle of the art scene. For one thing, in the fifties many dealers and collectors succumbed to the false notion that an artist in love with the visual world was hopelessly "atavistic," and thereby barred themselves and others from creations endowed with the same fervor and vitality as are many of the better nonfigurative, nonobjective paintings of the New York School and the San Francisco School. Indeed, such "atavists" often give more insight into the laws governing the making of significant form than do the Non-Objectivists. Filmus may have thought that, once having been accorded the recognition and love that are manna to an artist's soul, he was not starved for acknowledgment, and that if the leaders of the art world wished to be informed of what he had produced more recently, they could make the brief trip to the quiet of his studio in Great Neck and themselves "rediscover" him and the inherent solid qualities of his work.

At the same time, Filmus has refused to allow the obvious merits of his work to be

exploited in attacks on the equally obvious shortcomings of much fashionable art. Above all, he is not a foe of what, for lack of a more precise term, has been labeled "abstract art." He himself is abstract to the degree that pleases his mind's eye. Whether he draws or paints portraits of family and friends, musicians at work, art lovers at a *vernissage*, dancers resting from their routine, Chassidim studying or in conversation with each other, he takes away all nonessential visual data, filtering through his emotions the mass of material surrounding him. Nature is not an artist; people do not congregate in a gallery in accordance with the unwritten laws of perfect design. As a teacher, Filmus urges his students to do what he himself has been doing over the past three decades, to create order out of chaos. Design, as he knows and teaches it, means to him re-creation, arrived at by an emotionally achieved but carefully planned rearrangement, and even distortion, of all that nature reveals to the eye.

Yet he feels that he needs the recognizable human figure and man's all-expressive face, to communicate his spiritual and aesthetic messages. I am reminded of the harsh reaction of an earlier artist, the German sculptor Ernst Barlach, to the work of Kandinsky. In a letter to a friend, he wrote:

"… my artistic language is the human figure or the object through which or in which man lives, suffers, rejoices, feels, thinks…. The things that arrest my attention are what a human being has suffered and is able to endure, his greatness, his concerns…."

And he wrote further:

"… I should like to use a word that to you, as a student of Schopenhauer, will not be without significance: the word 'sympathy.' I need to feel a sense of sympathy, feel what others are feeling, suffer what they are suffering. And even where sympathy is out of place, then I sympathize with myself for being so inferior, so far from resembling those who may well feel sorry for me. Sympathy need not be doleful. I can sense it in the humorous as well as in the heroic. It could be expressed as the transfer of either pleasure or suffering. That is, taking them myself on the behalf of others. This sympathetic participation reaches the point where I find myself transported into the midst of the events visualized."

This letter was written half a century ago by a man with whom Filmus has little in common; little, that is, except for his profound humanity. As a Jew who spent part of his childhood in a Russian village, and who grew up in a milieu created here by Jewish refugees from Czarist oppression, Filmus often heard a word that to his ears may have a stronger, more familiar ring than sympathy. I am referring to *rachmones*, a term for which no single, real equivalent can be found in the English language. It stands for mercy, for pity, for compassion, and for a variety of other subtle expressions of the soul. The Jewish sages tell us that, in return for the mercy of God, man is expected to show mercy to his fellow men. Man is also expected to have pity, which in Jewish thought is regarded as one of the noblest

virtues. Such pity is not mere condescension but rather a feeling of kinship with all fellow creatures, and basically is the identification of one's self with another whose lot is less fortunate.

Noble sentiments alone, of course, do not create valid art. But they are no obstacle to the creation of such art. An artist can be a cynic, like Oscar Wilde or his fellow wit, the painter Whistler, and, despite a rather negative attitude toward humanity, can create works that command our respect even if they fail to penetrate to our hearts. Yet it is significant that the works by Wilde that are most likely to remain are those created in the last tragic years of his career, when suffering made him sling aside the multicolored coat of a jester. Whistler led the way toward abstract art by insisting that art should be "independent of all claptrap—should stand alone, and appeal to the artistic sense of eye or ear, without confounding this with emotions entirely foreign to it, as devotion, pity, love, patriotism, and the like." Yet, is his portrait of his mother—the one picture he managed to infuse with real filial love—nothing more than an *Arrangement in Grey and Black*?

Filmus believes that he has a duty to express through his art a spiritual message rather than occupy himself solely with problems of form. He does not believe that the various pigments, the surfaces of canvas, wood, metal, or stone should become ends in themselves. When Degas was asked what he was mixing his pigments with, he quipped, "With brain." While it is true that a painting is made with pigments and a poem with words, pigment- or word-obsession often omits the spirituality in man that alone lifts the handling of material from animal pleasure to the realm of art.

Filmus, if I may paraphrase Degas, mixes his rich, juicy pigments with *rachmones*. Years ago he made a statement to which he still subscribes:

"The artist creates a work of art; the purpose which underlies its making is expression, either personal or social. Inherent in the product is the personality of the artist. Art should be felt to be something growing out of the interests that supply driving force to our daily life, otherwise it will remain the object of concealed indifference on the part of the public and academic professionalism on the part of the artist."

His interests are confined. While he has drawn and painted landscapes, flowers, still lifes, his preoccupation is with people. There are his portraits, especially those of wife and children. Those who know and recognize the sitters feel, none the less, the imprint of the artist's interpretative mind. To those who never met the sitters, they are still meaningful as warm evocations, in delicate line or with a loaded brush, of the love binding a sensitive man to other equally responsive people. Samuel Johnson once wisely remarked, "Portrait painting is a reasonable and natural consequence of affection." This means, of course, that the best work is done whenever there exists an intimacy between the artist and the sitter, a strong personal bond uniting the two characters.

[17]

Next comes his infatuation with dancers. Gladys Nodiff, whom he married in 1939, remained a dancer for many years. What interested Filmus far more than the fleeting motion of the dance itself, however, were the personalities of the slim young women in tights, backstage, where they put on make-up, combed their hair, or simply relaxed in the most natural attitudes after the strain of action. Through his wife and her friends, he knew so well all the usual movements and postures of the dancers that he was able to summarize them as few painters have managed to do since Degas. Like Degas, he captures their forms, massed almost sculpturally against a neutral background, their grace expressing itself even in the faces, however abbreviated and summarized the treatment might be.

Musicians are another favorite theme: a man playing the violin, a small group gathered to produce chamber music, or a large orchestra under a leader. When Raoul Dufy painted orchestras, he was primarily attracted by the agitated movements of the musicians and

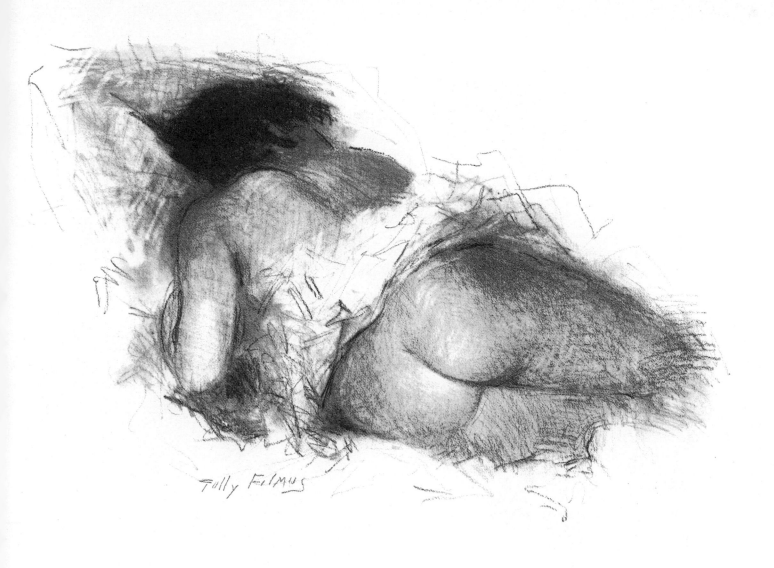

their instruments. Here, however, the stress is on the psychological penetration of the faces, even where each one occupies only a square inch or two on the canvas. As in the mature work of Rembrandt, who is Filmus' greatest idol, the head remains the focus of attention while the rest is deliberately blurred or stripped of all but the most essential traits.

Among his finest oils are the unconventional sketches—some of them very small—of people looking at pictures in museums or galleries. They are related to Daumier's connoisseurs visiting the Salon. They recall the statement of an 18th century German, Lichtenberg, who wrote, "Nothing hears as many silly remarks as a picture hanging in a gallery." With the same subtle sense of humor that prompted the work of Daumier, Filmus shows men and women viewing works of art with naïveté, puzzlement, or anger. Another of Daumier's themes is often treated by Filmus: the artist in the solitude of his studio, looking at his own work with a mixture of contentment and anxiety.

[19]

Again and again we are reminded, through the broad, cursory treatment of body and face, first of Daumier, and then of the later Rembrandt. It is not a coincidence that to a great many American artists who developed their craft in the Age of Depression, Rembrandt the humanist, the man of the people, the outsider, was a god. Chronologically midway between Weber and Baskin, Filmus belonged to the scores of painters and sculptors, immigrants or the children of immigrants, who enriched the American scene with Rembrandtesque work significant both socially and aesthetically. In the days of the WPA they were in the forefront of the movement known as Social Realism, which was preoccupied with artistic comment upon current political and economic conditions. They knew life's hard reality, for they did not receive allowances from their families, who were often poor, and often, as Tully's parents were not, opposed to their sons' pursuit of art. They worked indefatigably at menial jobs during the day to support themselves so as to be free in the evening to attend art school. Never before had the United States experienced a Depression so widespread and grim as that of the thirties, when, as President Roosevelt put it, a host of unemployed citizens were facing the dire problem of existence, while an equally great number were toiling with little return.

Filmus will not object to being called a product of that turbulent and tragic, yet fruitful, era that came to an end with Pearl Harbor and the war that changed the face of the nation. In the thirties, Filmus and men like Gropper, Shahn, Levine, the Soyers, and others who were on the WPA arts project, concerned themselves, in the tradition of earnest realistic art, with interpreting the essential nature of their subjects. The work of these men presents a rare mixture of Realism and Expressionism; the artists frequently resorted to spontaneous, intuitive distortions of the ordinary forms and colors of nature so as to achieve certain emotional or aesthetic effects.

Some of the men Filmus associated with in the thirties were to change their style either as a natural and logical development, or because it was the fashionable trend. Though Filmus' technique became freer, bolder, broader, more abstract in the course of years, his basic outlook on life and, therefore, the direction of his art have not changed. It is true that in the period mentioned above, slum areas, poverty-stricken farms, home relief offices, and other distressing sights were depicted, by not particularly gifted men, with too much fidelity to nature and insufficient concern for significant form. But the fact that much of the output of those years was sentimental, melodramatic, and even banal, did not lead Filmus—and must not lead us—to allow fickle taste to taboo all "storytelling," to outlaw any painting or sculpture that has intentional resemblance to figures or objects in the everyday world.

Filmus, though he is now a financially comfortable man in his mid-fifties, still refuses to share the foolish optimism of those whom the late Franklin D. Roosevelt once assailed because they would deny the "dark realities of the moment." The poor, sorrowful, alien Jew, who is now an infrequent sight on the streets of New York, lives on in many a painting by Filmus, a near-allegorical creature, an almost bewildering sight to a generation of self-satisfied cocktail sippers who prefer art that is decorative rather than expressive, as soothing and negligible as the background music to a cheerful, if rather superficial, conversation in a suburban living room.

Throughout all that has happened in the world of art, Filmus steadfastly has remained a humanist. His drawings and paintings cry out: All that matters is Man, what he has created, what he has suffered. In the highest sense of the term, he is a propagandist; his art transmits an individual's strong feelings about man and his world. In a country that is the epitome of activity and buoyancy, he dares to remind us that ours is an Age of Anxiety as much as it is an Age of Prosperity. With the lyrical beauty, the spiritual tranquillity that sings to us here in color and line, the deeper and more challenging aspects of life are never forgotten. Perhaps Filmus has lately concentrated so much on painting Jewish types because

Collection Mr. and Mrs. Abe Lerner

the homely old-time Jew, whatever else he may have been, was not a stereotype. It is highly refreshing and exciting to come across the work of a man who dares again to put Common Man, Everyman, in the center of a picture, and who does so with a simplicity and grandeur that can be attained only through many, many years of earnest, sincere struggle in the loneliness of a studio.

Tully Filmus

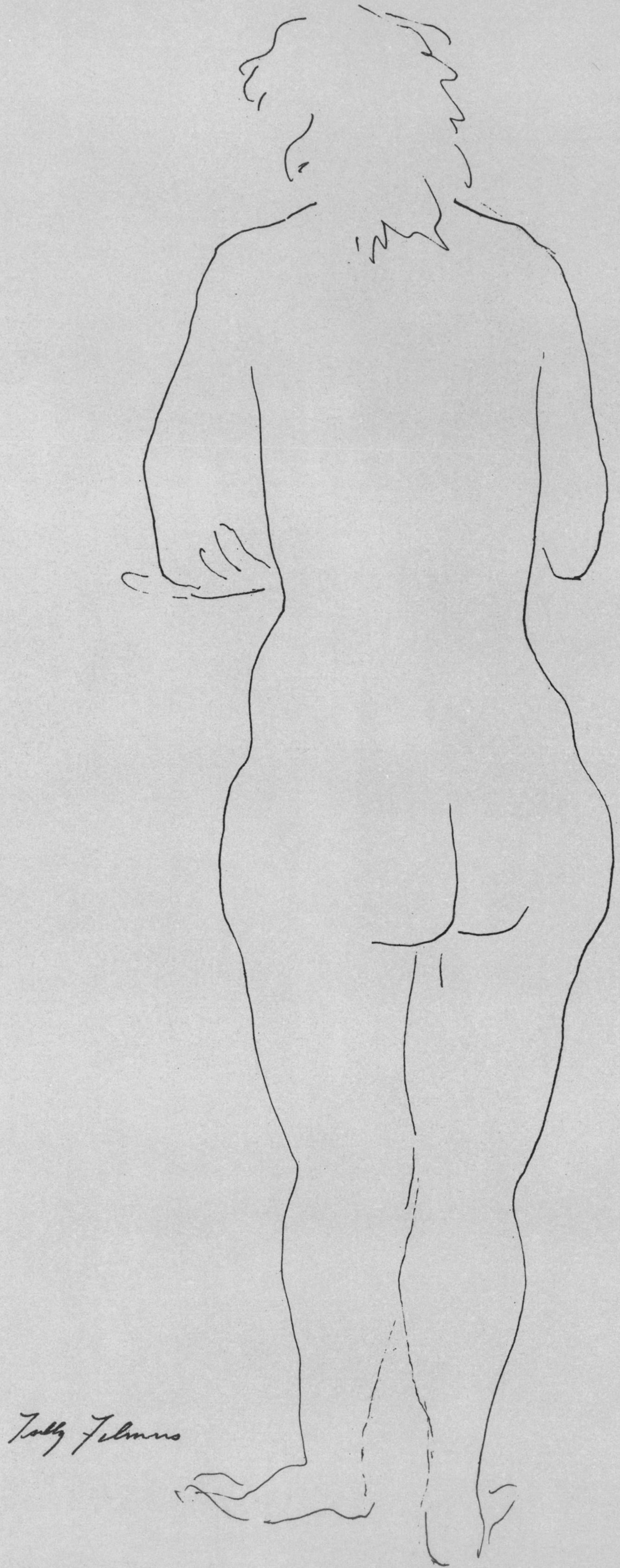

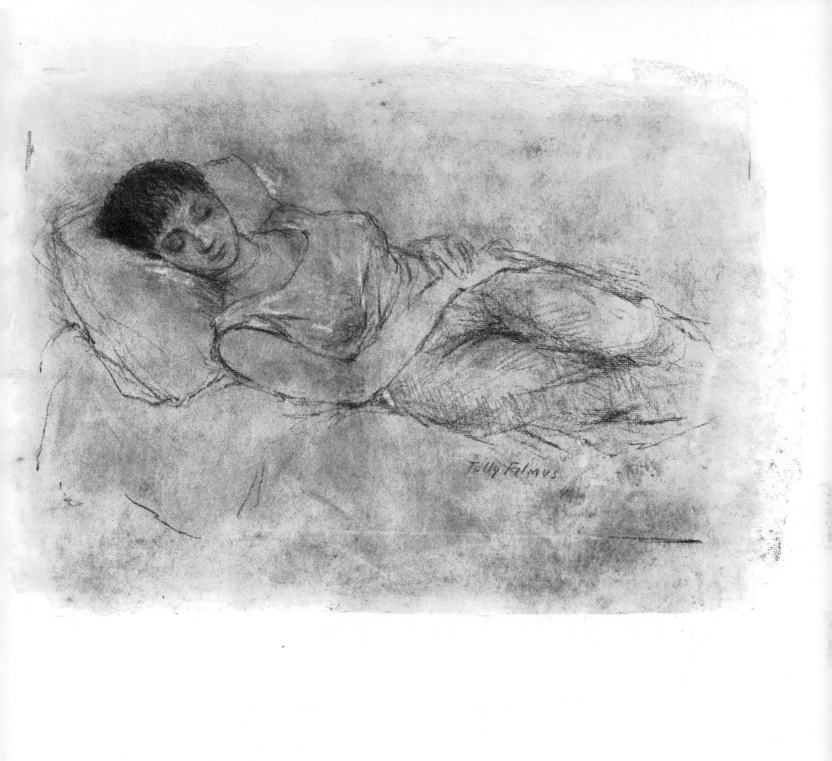

Trudy Fehrman

Tully Filmus
1935

Tully Filmus

CHRONOLOGY

1908   August 29. Born Anatol (Tully) Filmus in Ataki, Bessarabia, son of Michael and Eva Filmus.

1913   Family came to United States, settled in Philadelphia.
        Tully attended Belmont Grammar School.

1920-24   Evening art classes at Graphic Sketch Club of Fleisher Art Foundation.

1921-24   Central High School. During this period he painted portraits of his teachers; commissioned
        by Mary Gaston Barnwell Foundation to paint portrait of founder, James G. Barnwell.

1924-27   Awarded scholarship to and studied at Pennsylvania Academy of the Fine Arts under Henry
        McCarter.

1925-27   Attended seminars at the Barnes Foundation in Merion, Pa. There met Jules Pascin and
        John Dewey. First saw paintings by Cézanne, Matisse, Picasso, Renoir.

1927   Pennsylvania Academy of the Fine Arts awarded him Cresson Traveling Scholarship for
        study abroad.

1927-29   Secured a studio in Paris in the Rue du Renne. Studies with André Lhôte. Worked independ-
        ently in Florence, Rome, Venice, Munich.

1930   Came to New York—took job with small art agency where he met and became a friend
        of Anton Refregier and Willem de Kooning.

1934   Returned to Europe (England, U.S.S.R., France).
        Studied works of the masters.

1935   Fleisher Art Foundation purchased painting from Art Alliance Exhibition, Philadelphia, Pa.

1936   Worked on the Federal Arts Project of the WPA.
        Joined American artists in contributing painting to Biro-Bidjan Museum, U.S.S.R.

1937   Exhibited at American Artists Congress.

1937-39   On faculty of American Artists School.

1938-50   Taught painting, drawing, and anatomy at the Cooper Union School of Art.

1939   June 18. Married Gladys Nodiff.

1940   Exhibited in the Whitney Museum Annual, and American Artists Congress.
        Painting of his acquired by permanent collection, New York University.

[46]

1941   Exhibited: Carnegie Institute, Whitney Museum Annual, Art Institute of Chicago, Corcoran Gallery in Washington, D.C., American Federation of Art Traveling Show.

1942   Exhibited: Pennsylvania Academy of the Fine Arts, Whitney Museum Annual, Carnegie Institute, Art Institute of Chicago, Denver Art Museum, State University of Iowa.

1943   May 12. Birth of son, Michael Roy.
Exhibited: Whitney Museum Annual, Pennsylvania Academy of the Fine Arts, Art Institute of Chicago, San Francisco Museum of Art, University of Texas.

1944   Joint purchase of painting by Metropolitan Museum of Art and Whitney Museum of American Art from Whitney Museum Annual.
Exhibited: Carnegie Institute, City Art Museum of St. Louis.

1945   Exhibited: Pennsylvania Academy of the Fine Arts, Whitney Museum Annual, Audubon Artists.

1946   Exhibited: Whitney Museum, Carnegie Institute, City Art Museum of St. Louis.

1947   Exhibited: Carnegie Institute, Toledo Museum of Art. Member of Artists Equity Association, Audubon Artists, Fellowship of Pennsylvania Academy of the Fine Arts.

1948   February 4. Birth of second son, Stephen Isaac.
Exhibited Pennsylvania Academy. Awarded Fellowship Prize by Pennsylvania Academy.
Painting acquired by permanent collection, Tel-Aviv Museum.

1951   Exhibited Brooklyn Museum. Permanent collection, Ein-Harod Museum, Israel.

1952   Permanent collection, Tel-Aviv Museum.

1953   Permanent collection, Massachusetts Institute of Technology, Cambridge, Mass.

1957   Spring. Traveled in France and Italy.

1961   Joined ACA Gallery, New York.

1963   Exhibited Queens College, New York.
One-man show ACA Gallery, New York.

THE PAINTINGS

3. SELF—PORTRAIT. 1963. 20 X 26. COLLECTION OF THE ARTIST.

All paintings are oil on canvas.
Dimensions are given in inches, height first.
The photographs from which the paintings
are reproduced were taken by Colten, New York.

4. SELF-PORTRAIT. 1925. 17 X 13. COLLECTION OF THE ARTIST.

5. LITTLE BOY. 1928. 16 x 20. BIRO-BIDJAN MUSEUM.

6. THE REDHEAD. 1928. 20 X 16. COLLECTION OF THE ARTIST.

7. ROCKPORT. 1938. 24 x 30. COLLECTION DR. AND MRS. JACK ROSEN.

8. PRIMPING. 1935. 30 x 24. COLLECTION OF THE ARTIST.

9. THE BATHERS. 1940. 11 x 14. ACA GALLERY.

10. TWO DANCERS. 1959. 16 x 12. COLLECTION MR. AND MRS. JOSEPH RESNICK.

11. THE NEW HAT. 1942. 30 X 24. COLLECTION GLADYS FILMUS.

12. BRICKLAYERS. 1940. 24 X 30. ACA GALLERY.

13. PORTRAIT OF FRANCIS CRISS. 1939. 30 X 24. COLLECTION OF THE ARTIST.

14. THE REDHEAD. 1943. 14 X 11. ACA GALLERY.

15. CONTEMPLATION. 1943. 10 X 8. COLLECTION DR. AND MRS. NORMAN AVNET.

16. POSING. 1940. 30 x 24. COLLECTION GLADYS FILMUS.

17. GLADYS. 1944. 30 x 24. COLLECTION OF THE WHITNEY MUSEUM OF AMERICAN ART.

18. THE OLD CARPENTER. 1947. 53 X 29. COLLECTION MR. AND MRS. LESTER AVNET.

19. THE OLD CARPENTER. DETAIL.

20. THE TEACHER. 1947. 15 X 10. ACA GALLERY.

21. GIRL IN PINK. 1947. 34 x 26. COLLECTION MR. AND MRS. HERBERT PHILIPS.

22. RESTING. 1945. 16 x 13. COLLECTION OF THE ARTIST.

Tully Filmus

23. SKETCH CLASS. 1947. 24 X 14. ACA GALLERY.

24. THE SCULPTOR. 1950. 32 X 16. ACA GALLERY.

25. GIRL IN THE MIRROR. 1951. 10 X 12. COLLECTION MR. AND MRS. GERALD LIGHT.

26. ALICE. 1952. 16 X 12. ACA GALLERY.

27. VIOLINIST. 1950. 18 X 28. COLLECTION MR. AND MRS. LESTER AVNET.

28. DEMONSTRATION. 1945. 52 x 30. COLLECTION MR. AND MRS. LESTER AVNET.

29. FLOWERED HAT. 1953. 14 X 11. COLLECTION MR. AND MRS. DAVID NELSON.

30. THE RED SWEATER. 1954. 14 X 11. COLLECTION GLADYS FILMUS.

31. TWO GIRLS. 1954. 17 X 13. COLLECTION MR. AND MRS. REUBEN L. KERSHAW.

32. DRESSING. 1954. 13 X 22. COLLECTION DR. AND MRS. EUGENE SALAND.

33. AT THE MUSEUM. 1954. 30 X 16. ACA GALLERY.

34. THE FLUTE PLAYER. 1956. 11 x 14. COLLECTION DR. AND MRS. ARTHUR S. CARLSON.

35. MUSIC MAKERS. 1955. 20 X 26. COLLECTION MR. AND MRS. ARNOLD ROSENBERG.

36. GOSSIPS. 1956. 16 X 20. ACA GALLERY.

37. GIRL ON CHAIR. 1954. 10 X 18. COLLECTION GLADYS FILMUS.

38. GIRL READING. 1957. 14 X 11. ACA GALLERY.

39. APRIL. 1955. 14 X 30. COLLECTION MR. AND MRS. JOSEPH RESNICK.

40. RAIN. 1956. 22 X 12. COLLECTION DR. AND MRS. SIDNEY SAMIS.

41. EXHIBITION OPENING. 1957. 20 X 26. COLLECTION DR. AND MRS. NORMAN AVNET.

42. SUNDAY IN THE MUSEUM. 1957. 16 X 30. COLLECTION MR. AND MRS. ARTHUR P. GOULD.

43. GIRL IN BLUE. 1958. 30 X 14. COLLECTION CHARLES AVNET.

44. THREE GIRLS. 1957. 10 x 8. COLLECTION MR. AND MRS. AL SCHWARTZ.

45. AT THE GALLERY. 1958. 16 X 20. COLLECTION MR. AND MRS. SEYMOUR KLEINMAN.

46. NORA. 1958. 34 x 23. ACA GALLERY.

47. STOOPED OLD MAN. 1959. 24 X 14. ACA GALLERY.

48. SUMMER RAIN. 1958. 13 x 24. COLLECTION MR. AND MRS. MARTIN C. BARELL.

49. CLOWN. 1957. 14 X 11. COLLECTION JONATHAN AVNET.

50. ARTIST'S WIFE. 1960. 24 × 14. COLLECTION OF THE ARTIST.

51. LISA. 1959. 34 X 20. COLLECTION MR. AND MRS. LESTER AVNET.

52. PRETZEL VENDOR. 1959. 14 X 11. COLLECTION CHAIM SHURSHA.

53. WOMAN ON BALCONY. 1959. 30 x 16. COLLECTION MR. AND MRS. SAM MARKS.

54. GIOVANNA. 1960. 14 X 11. ACA GALLERY.

55. CIRCUS GIRL. 1963. 30 X 20. ACA GALLERY.

56. BACKSTAGE. 1958. 30 X 40. COLLECTION MR. AND MRS. LESTER AVNET.

57. DRESSING ROOM. 1960. 26 X 36. COLLECTION MR. AND MRS. LESTER AVNET.

58. THE HORA. 1958. 34 X 23. COLLECTION DR. AND MRS. JACK ROSEN.

59. READING ROOM. 1959. 20 X 30. ACA GALLERY.

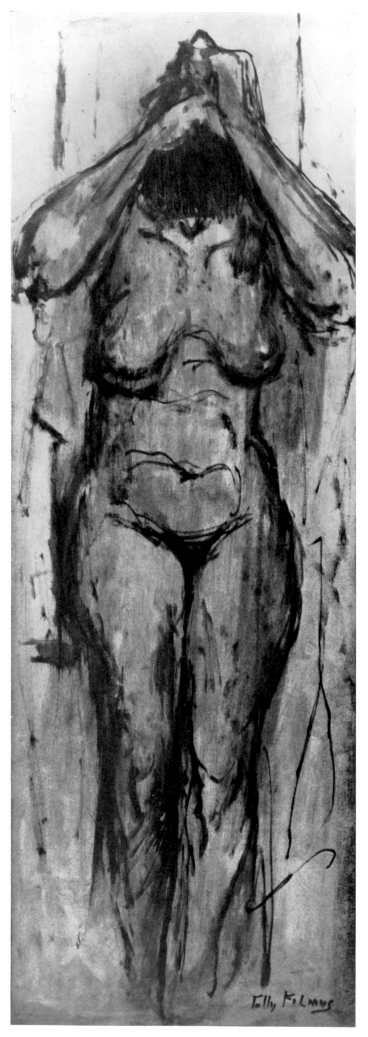

60. NUDE. 1959. 34 X 12. ACA GALLERY.

61. AFTER WORK. 1959. 26 x 10. ACA GALLERY.

62. OLD FRIENDS. 1960. 20 X 14. COLLECTION MR. AND MRS. BORIS M. TARNA.

63. MORNING PAPER. 1960. 24 x 14. ACA GALLERY.

64. THE DISCUSSION. 1962. 29 X 14. COLLECTION DR. AND MRS. NORMAN AVNET.

65. CHASSIDIC DANCE. 1961. 36 x 28. COLLECTION DR. AND MRS. NORMAN AVNET.

66. POINT OF INFORMATION. 1961. 16 X 30. ACA GALLERY.

67. PATRIARCH. 1961. 26 x 10. COLLECTION
DR. AND MRS. NORMAN AVNET.

68. MICHAEL. 1962. 20 x 14. COLLECTION MICHAEL ROY FILMUS.

69. STEPHEN. 1961. 20 x 14. COLLECTION STEPHEN ISAAC FILMUS.

70. THE RETURN. 1962. 26 x 12. ACA GALLERY.

71. PRESERVING THE TORAH. 1962. 23 X 34. ACA GALLERY.

72. CHAMBER MUSIC. 1962. 36 x 26. ACA GALLERY.

73. TRIO. 1962. 30 X 40. ACA GALLERY.

74. THE KLEZMER. 1961. 26 x 32. COLLECTION MR. AND MRS. LESTER AVNET.

75. THE ORCHESTRA. 1962. 30 X 40. COLLECTION MR. AND MRS. LESTER AVNET.

76. AT THE PIANO. 1962. 14 X 19. COLLECTION MR. AND MRS. LESTER AVNET.

77. PRINT COLLECTOR. 1962. 24 x 20. COLLECTION DR. AND MRS. THEODORE ROBERTSON.

78. CONNOISSEUR. 1961. 13 X 6. COLLECTION OF THE ARTIST.

79. THE CONCERT. 1961. 30 x 40. COLLECTION MR. AND MRS. ROBERT H. AVNET.

80. THE VILLAGE. 1963. 30 X 50. ACA GALLERY.

81. OLD SCHOLAR. 1963. 10 x 8. COLLECTION OF THE ARTIST.

A Comprehensive List of Paintings by Tully Filmus

1925   Self-Portrait. 17 x 13. Collection of the artist. (Pl. 4)

1928   Little Boy. 16 x 20. Biro-Bidjan Museum, U.S.S.R. (Pl. 5)

Figure. 30 x 24. Mary Gaston Barnwell Foundation, Philadelphia, Pa.

Portrait of Dr. John Lewis Haney. 40 x 30. Central High School, Philadelphia, Pa.

The Redhead. 20 x 16. Collection of the artist. (Pl. 6)

Old Woman with Hat. 20 x 16. Collection of the artist.

1929   Woman with Mandolin. 30 x 24. Collection Mr. and Mrs. Philip Rothman, Newark, N.J.

Still Life. 30 x 24. Collection Mr. and Mrs. Irving Feltman, Brooklyn, N.Y.

The Actor. 24 x 20. Collection Mr. and Mrs. Julius Gordon, Philadelphia, Pa.

Oak Trees. 30 x 22. Collection Mr. and Mrs. Ernest L. Broder, Camden, N.J.

1930   Woodstock. 24 x 20. Collection of the artist.

The Straw Hat. 26 x 22. Collection Mr. and Mrs. Henry Bauer, New York.

The Orchard. 22 x 28. Collection Mr. and Mrs. Richard Glasner, New York.

Fantasy. 30 x 24. Collection Dr. and Mrs. Harry L. Stein, New York.

1931   New York Roof Tops. 24 x 32. Collection Mr. and Mrs. Martin Hollander, New York.

The Spectators. 24 x 20. Collection Mr. and Mrs. Robert L. Friedland, New York.

Dance Group. 24 x 30. Collection Mr. and Mrs. Philip Davidson, New York.

Oboe Player. 20 x 16. Collection of the artist.

The Bridge. 22 x 28. Collection Mr. and Mrs. William E. Burke, Boston, Mass.

Cellist. 30 x 24. Collection Dr. and Mrs. Nathan Stern, Philadelphia, Pa.

1932   Dancers. 32 x 26. Collection Mr. and Mrs. Herbert Linton, Richmond, Va.

Self-Portrait. 24 x 20. Collection of the artist.

Winter. 26 x 22. Collection Mr. and Mrs. Mitchell Rittenberg, New York.

The Spectators. 20 x 26. Collection of the artist.

Fantasy. 30 x 22. Collection Dr. and Mrs. Jacob Fishman, Philadelphia, Pa.

1934   Masquerade. 34 x 30. Collection Mr. and Mrs. Harry L. Marcus, Boston, Mass.

Self-Portrait. 30 x 24. Collection of the artist.

Men Working. 32 x 24. Collection Mr. and Mrs. Bernard Gross, New York.

Barn in Woodstock. 24 x 28. Collection Mr. and Mrs. Martin L. Spalding, Hollywood, Calif.

Reclining Figure. 24 x 32. Collection Mr. and Mrs. Henry Littman, New York.

Dancers. 28 x 22. Collection Mr. and Mrs. Emanuel Hartman, Philadelphia, Pa.

1935   Primping. 30 x 24. Collection of the artist. (Pl. 8)

Adolescence. 36 x 26. Fleisher Art Foundation, Philadelphia, Pa.

In the Park. 26 x 34. Collection Mr. and Mrs. Theodore L. Mayer, New York.

Jobless. 38 x 26. Collection Dr. and Mrs. Benjamin Lambert, Lynn, Mass.

Still Life. 24 x 20. Collection of the artist.

Acrobats. 16 x 28. Collection Mr. and Mrs. Joseph Redman, Washington, D.C.

Children at Play. 24 x 30. Collection of the artist.

After the Performance. 30 x 36. Collection Mr. and Mrs. David Wollman, Washington, D.C.

1936   Children. 24 x 30. Abraham Lincoln High School, Brooklyn, N.Y.

Seated at the Mirror. 30 x 24. Collection Mr. and Mrs. Oscar Steinberg, Greenwich, Conn.

Figures. 20 x 24. James Monroe High School, Bronx, N.Y.

Dancer Resting. 30 x 22. Collection Mr. and Mrs. David Kingman, Chicago, Ill.

Abduction. 20 x 16. Collection Dr. and Mrs. Herman A. Stein, Morristown, N.J.

On Stage. 20 x 24. Alexander Hamilton High School, Brooklyn, N.Y.

1937   Girl Combing Her Hair. 30 x 24. Collection Mr. and Mrs. Harris Stone, Silver Spring, Md.

Roof Tops. 24 x 20. Collection Mr. and Mrs. Philip Dorfman, Jersey City, N.J.

City Street. 24 x 36. Collection Mr. and Mrs. Daniel Stone, New York.

Reading. 24 x 20. James Monroe High School, Bronx, N.Y.

Choirboy. 44 x 30. Collection Miss Pauline Fraser, New York.

The Flowered Hat. 20 x 24. Collection Mr. and Mrs. Martin L. Spector, Lynn, Mass.

1938   Dancer in Blue. 30 x 24. Collection Dr. and Mrs. Jacob A. Nathans, Chicago, Ill.

Village Street. 20 x 28. Portchester High School, Portchester, N.Y.

Self-Portrait. 30 x 24. Collection of the artist.

Young Girl. 24 x 20. Collection Mr. and Mrs. Paul Baskin, Rye, N.Y.

Rockport. 24 x 30. Collection Dr. and Mrs. Jack Rosen, Brooklyn, N.Y. (Pl. 7)

Still Life. 22 x 28. Alexander Hamilton High School, Brooklyn, N.Y.

The Bridge. 26 x 30. General Hospital, Washington, D.C.

New England Barn. 26 x 32. Collection Mr. and Mrs. Lewis Landis, New York.

1939   Ballerinas. 20 x 16. Collection Mr. and Mrs. Sol Furman, Brooklyn, N.Y.

Norma. 36 x 30. Collection Mr. and Mrs. Meyer Shein, Williston, N.Y.

Gladys. 30 x 24. Collection Dr. and Mrs. Norman Avnet, Great Neck, N.Y. (Pl. 1)

Portrait of Francis Criss. 30 x 24. Collection of the artist. (Pl. 13)

Gladys. 30 x 24. Collection Miss Ida Roth, Brooklyn, N.Y.

Anemones. 20 x 26. Collection Dr. and Mrs. Jack Rosen, Brooklyn, N.Y.

Figure in White. 30 x 24. Collection Mr. and Mrs. Lewis Schecter, Montreal, Canada.

Posing. 10 x 8. Collection Mr. and Mrs. Samuel J. Goldberg, Brooklyn, N.Y.

Portrait of M. Zabnitsky. 40 x 30. New York Historical Society, New York.

Trees. 15 x 25. Collection Mr. and Mrs. Julius Vogel, Brooklyn, N.Y.

1940   Posing. 30 x 24. Collection Gladys Filmus. (Pl. 16)

Nina. 32 x 26. New York University, New York.

My Wife. 36 x 30. Collection of the artist.

Flowers. 24 x 20. Collection Mr. and Mrs. Sol Furman, Brooklyn, N.Y.

Horse and Wagon. 26 x 36. Collection Mr. and Mrs. Lester Avnet, Kings Point, N.Y. (Pl. 2)

Bricklayers. 24 x 30. ACA Gallery, New York. (Pl. 12)

Young Girl with Cat. 30 x 22. Collection Dr. and Mrs. Mark L. Steller, Boston, Mass.

After the Rehearsal. 38 x 26. Collection Mr. and Mrs. Leonard Cooper, Chicago, Ill.

The Bathers. 11 x 14. ACA Gallery, New York. (Pl. 9)

1941   Sisters. 28 x 24. Collection Mr. and Mrs. Nathan Schechter, Bronxville, N.Y.

Still Life. 36 x 30. Collection Mr. and Mrs. Nathan Schechter, Bronxville, N.Y.

Portrait of Julian Levy. 30 x 24. Collection of the artist.

Wild Flowers. 22 x 10. Collection Miss Ida Roth, Brooklyn, N.Y.

On the Park Bench. 20 x 26. Collection Mr. and Mrs. Richard Moore, Philadelphia, Pa.

Men Working. 36 x 28. Collection Dr. and Mrs. Ezra Lipsky, Lynn, Mass.

1942   Provincetown. 25 x 30. Collection Dr. and Mrs. Harry A. Mackler, Brooklyn, N.Y.

Backstage. 24 x 30. Collection Mrs. Barkley McKee Henry, New York.

The New Hat. 30 x 24. Collection Gladys Filmus. (Pl. 11)

Richard. 20 x 16. Collection Mr. and Mrs. Alfredo Valente, New York.

The Window. 30 x 22. Collection Fleisher Art Foundation, Philadelphia, Pa.

Waiting. 26 x 22. Collection Dr. and Mrs. Carl Lawton, Syracuse, N.Y.

In the Park. 26 x 32. Andrew Foundation, Chicago, Ill.

Winter Landscape. 24 x 36. Collection Dr. and Mrs. Edward C. Cooper, Greenwich, Conn.

Renee and Mimi. 12 inches diameter, tondo. Collection Mr. and Mrs. Chaim Gross, New York.

1943   Mimi. 30 x 24. Collection Mr. and Mrs. Theodore Kirchenbaum, Jersey City, N.J.

Contemplation. 10 x 8. Collection Dr. and Mrs. Norman Avnet, Great Neck, N.Y. (Pl. 15)

Seated Figure. 36 x 26. Collection Mr. and Mrs. Louis Schindler, Forest Hills, N.Y.

Locust Trees. 28 x 21. Collection Dr. and Mrs. Myron Herman, Yonkers, N.Y.

Backstage. 24 x 32. Collection Mrs. Henry Whitney, New York.

Children. 28 x 32. Collection Mr. and Mrs. Harry Merdinger, Mount Vernon, N.Y.

Before the Performance. 24 x 32. Collection Dr. and Mrs. John Porges, Forest Hills, N.Y.

The Redhead. 14 x 11. ACA Gallery, New York. (Pl. 14)

1944   Gladys. 30 x 24. Collection of the Whitney Museum of American Art, New York. (Pl. 17)

Acrobats. 20 x 28. Collection Mr. and Mrs. Albert H. Jensen, Washington, D.C.

Laurence. 18 x 15. Collection Mr. and Mrs. Bernard Fink, West Hempstead, N.Y.

Woman in Blue. 34 x 28. Collection Dr. and Mrs. Jack Rosen, Brooklyn, N.Y.

The Children. 34 x 26. Collection Dr. and Mrs. Jack Rosen, Brooklyn, N.Y.

Resting. 24 x 30. Collection Miss Ida Roth, Brooklyn, N.Y.

Summer Afternoon. 26 x 22. Collection Mr. and Mrs. Eliot Lang, Ithaca, N.Y.

Farmers. 28 x 22. Collection Mr. and Mrs. Sidney B. Ullman, Hollywood, Calif.

Woodstock Barn. 20 x 26. Collection Mr. and Mrs. Paul C. Wilson, Tenafly, N.J.

Figure. 40 x 30. Collection Mr. and Mrs. Abe Meltzer, Kings Point, N.Y.

1945   Resting. 16 x 13. Collection of the artist. (Pl. 22)

Gray Day. 16 x 20. Collection Dr. and Mrs. Harry A. Mackler, Brooklyn, N.Y.

Rockport. 20 x 26. Collection Mr. and Mrs. Jerry G. Gonick, Silver Spring, Md.

Michael. 10 x 8. Collection Michael Roy Filmus.

Demonstration. 52 x 30. Collection Mr. and Mrs. Lester Avnet, Kings Point, N.Y. (Pl. 28)

Dance Rehearsal. 32 x 26. Collection Mr. and Mrs. Albert Bell, Toronto, Canada.

1946   Small Boats. 12 x 22. Collection Dr. and Mrs. Harry A. Mackler, Brooklyn, N.Y.

Fishermen. 18 x 22. Collection Dr. and Mrs. Harry A. Mackler, Brooklyn, N.Y.

Portrait of Ted Lewis. 36 x 30. Collection Mr. and Mrs. Ted Lewis, New York.

Adah. 36 x 30. Collection Mr. and Mrs. Ted Lewis, New York.

The Beach. 18 x 30. Collection Dr. and Mrs. Jack Rosen, Brooklyn, N.Y.

Provincetown. 26 x 22. Collection Dr. and Mrs. Leonard Kaufman, Manhattan Beach, N.Y.

Young Woman. 20 x 16. Collection Mr. and Mrs. Norman Hirschl, New York.

Primping. 30 x 24. Collection Mr. and Mrs. Donald Kagin, New York.

Procession. 22 x 30. Collection Mr. and Mrs. Walter P. Frank, Burbank, Calif.

1947   The Old Carpenter. 53 x 29. Collection Mr. and Mrs. Lester Avnet, Kings Point, N.Y. (Pl. 18 and 19)

At the Window. 32 x 25. Collection Mr. and Mrs. Bernard Fink, West Hempstead, N.Y.

Winter. 18 x 30. Collection Mr. and Mrs. Albert Merzon, Kew Gardens Hills, N.Y.

Bedtime. 12 x 16. Collection Mr. and Mrs. Barney Rosenstein, Cedarhurst, N.Y.

Figures. 30 x 24. Brooks Foundation, Chicago, Ill.

Child Reading. 24 x 20. Collection Mr. and Mrs. Stanley Hoffman, New York.

The Family. 36 x 30. Collection Mr. and Mrs. Ben Levin, Cedarhurst, N.Y.

Girl in Pink. 34 x 26. Collection Mr. and Mrs. Herbert Philips, Toledo, Ohio. (Pl. 21)

Sketch Class. 24 x 14. ACA Gallery, New York. (Pl. 23)

The Teacher. 15 x 10. ACA Gallery, New York. (Pl. 20)

Seated Figure. 36 x 30. Collection Mr. and Mrs. S. L. Hoffman, New York.

1948   Circus. 20 x 26. Collection Mr. and Mrs. Bertram Long, Chicago, Ill.

Farmers. 26 x 16. Tel-Aviv Museum, Israel.

Two Figures. 36 x 28. Collection Mr. and Mrs. A. A. Krejtman, New York.

Poppies. 16 x 20. Collection Dr. and Mrs. Herbert B. Goldman, Rockville Center, N.Y.

Girl in Pink. 32 x 14. Collection Dr. and Mrs. William D. Franklin, Great Neck, N.Y.

Barbara. 34 x 28. Collection Mr. and Mrs. Melvin Kass, New Hyde Park, N.Y.

Winter. 6 x 12. Collection Mr. and Mrs. Lewis Jacobs, Great Neck, N.Y.

Figure. 34 x 22. Collection Mr. and Mrs. Ben Koehl, Kings Point, N.Y.

1949   Boys. 20 x 16. Collection Mr. and Mrs. Joseph Resnick, Lawrence, N.Y.

Seated Figure. 34 x 28. Collection Mr. and Mrs. Joseph Resnick, Lawrence, N.Y.

Ballerinas. 14 x 23. Collection Mr. and Mrs. Louis Feldman, Woodmere, N.Y.

Joseph. 24 x 20. Collection Mr. and Mrs. Joseph Resnick, Lawrence, N.Y.

Mitchel Fields. 24 x 20. National Academy, New York.

Reading. 10 x 8. Collection Mr. and Mrs. Lester Avnet, Kings Point, N.Y.

Hired Hands. 22 x 12. Collection Mr. and Mrs. Louis Feldman, Woodmere, N.Y.

Masquerade. 24 x 32. Collection Mr. and Mrs. Irving Panzer, Kings Point, N.Y.

Haas Family. 34 x 28. Collection Mr. and Mrs. Raymond N. Haas, Long Beach, N.Y.

The Garden. 36 x 29. Collection Mr. and Mrs. Eugene A. Stonehill, Great Neck, N.Y.

My Wife. 36 x 30. Collection of the artist.

1950   Barbara. 40 x 30. Collection Mr. and Mrs. Max Axelrod, Lawrence, N.Y.

Connoisseur. 14 x 11. Collection Mr. and Mrs. Julius Vogel, Brooklyn, N.Y.

Portrait of Dr. Nathan D. Wilensky. 33 x 27. Collection Mrs. Ruth Wilensky, Brooklyn, N.Y.

Daniel and Edda. 30 x 24. Collection Mrs. Ruth Wilensky, Brooklyn, N.Y.

Ruth. 33 x 27. Collection Mrs. Ruth Wilensky, Brooklyn, N.Y.

Joan. 36 x 30. Collection Mr. and Mrs. Harry Levick, Forest Hills, N.Y.

The Sculptor. 32 x 16. ACA Gallery, New York. (Pl. 24)

Violinist. 18 x 28. Collection Mr. and Mrs. Lester Avnet, Kings Point, N.Y. (Pl. 27)

Portrait of Mark A. McCloskey. 37 x 29. Collection Mr. and Mrs. Mark A. McCloskey, New York.

Don Quixote. 34 x 24. Collection Mr. and Mrs. Irving Panzer, Kings Point, N.Y.

Early Morning. 16 x 30. Collection Mr. and Mrs. Oscar Abrin, Ormond Beach, Fla.

1951   Ruth. 32 x 26. Collection Dr. and Mrs. Hyman Friedman, Brooklyn, N.Y.

Big Business. 32 x 22. Collection Dr. and Mrs. Alexander Levine, Brooklyn, N.Y.

Elizabeth. 18 x 15. Collection Mr. and Mrs. Bernard Fink, West Hempstead, N.Y.

Girl in the Mirror. 10 x 12. Collection Mr. and Mrs. Gerald Light, Kings Point, N.Y. (Pl. 25)

Dance Group. 24 x 20. Collection Mr. and Mrs. Albert Merzon, Kew Gardens Hills, N.Y.

At Home. 32 x 36. Collection Mr. and Mrs. Richard Danberg, Rego Park, N.Y.

Bikini. 14 x 11. Collection Mr. and Mrs. Richard Roaman, Roslyn, N.Y.

Little Girl with a Mirror. 34 x 20. Collection Mr. and Mrs. Lester Avnet, Kings Point, N.Y.

Mother and Children. 10 x 18. Collection Mr. and Mrs. Louis Feldman, Woodmere, N.Y.

Ann. 34 x 26. Collection Mr. and Mrs. Adolph Levey, Philadelphia, Pa.

Countryside. 30 x 58. Collection Dr. and Mrs. Myron Herman, Yonkers, N.Y.

Bacchanal. 22 x 14. Collection Dr. and Mrs. Herbert B. Goldman, Rockville Center, N.Y.

Figure. 36 x 32. Collection Mr. and Mrs. Harvey Schiff, Hewlitt Harbor, N.Y.

Surf Fishing. 12 x 29. Collection Mr. and Mrs. Irving Panzer, Kings Point, N.Y.

Head. 10 x 8. Collection Mr. and Mrs. Stanley Swerdlow, Great Neck, N.Y.

Mother and Children. 42 x 32. Collection Mr. and Mrs. Harvey Schiff, Hewlitt Harbor, N.Y.

Family. 20 x 24. Ein-Harod Museum, Israel.

1952   New England. 13 x 35. Collection Mr. and Mrs. Theodore Bergman, Great Neck, N.Y.

Girl Resting. 10 x 8. Collection Mr. and Mrs. Gerald Light, Kings Point, N.Y.

Figure. 34 x 30. Collection Mr. and Mrs. David B. Rosen, Cedarhurst, N.Y.

David. 32 x 28. Collection Mr. and Mrs. David B. Rosen, Cedarhurst, N.Y.

Contemplation. 36 x 30. Collection Mr. and Mrs. Joseph Dansig, Hewlitt, N.Y.

Figure. 30 x 24. Collection Mr. and Mrs. David B. Rosen, Cedarhurst, N.Y.

Zina. 24 x 20. Collection Mr. and Mrs. Norman Auslander, New York.

Elissa. 24 x 20. Collection Mr. and Mrs. Alvin Burach, New York.

Two Figures. 32 x 26. Collection Mr. and Mrs. Bernard Feldman, New York.

Maralyn. 24 x 20. Collection Mr. and Mrs. Herbert Paer, Tenafly, N.J.

Woman in the Train. 20 x 14. Collection Mr. and Mrs. Robert W. Avnet, Los Angeles, Calif.

Masquerade. 18 x 46. Collection Mr. and Mrs. Eugene A. Stonehill, Great Neck, N.Y.

Young Woman. 30 x 24. Collection Mr. and Mrs. Walter Krinsky, Woodmere, N.Y.

Laura. 30 x 24. Collection Mr. and Mrs. Max Gonick, Brooklyn, N.Y.

Hay Pitching. 28 x 16. Tel-Aviv Museum, Israel.

Alice. 16 x 12. ACA Gallery, New York. (Pl. 26)

Mother and Child. 10 x 12. Collection Mr. and Mrs. Solomon M. Malkin, New York.

1953   Janice. 30 x 24. Collection Mr. and Mrs. David Feiner, Great Neck, N.Y.

Backstage. 32 x 26. Collection Mr. and Mrs. Michael Honig, Manhasset, N.Y.

Ballet. 14 x 32. Collection Mr. and Mrs. Benjamin Katz, Great Neck, N.Y.

Mother and Child. 16 x 8. Collection Dr. and Mrs. Irwin Kleinman, Brooklyn, N.Y.

Stanley Jay. 30 x 24. Collection Mr. and Mrs. Nathan Lagin, Great Neck, N.Y.

Flowered Hat. 14 x 11. Collection Mr. and Mrs. David Nelson, Woodmere, N.Y. (Pl. 29)

Ruth. 36 x 30. Collection Mr. and Mrs. David Schildiner, Jamaica Estates, N.Y.

Stanley and Sandra. 30 x 24. Collection Mr. and Mrs. David Schildiner, Jamaica Estates, N.Y.

Gladys. 20 x 16. Collection Mr. and Mrs. Robert H. Avnet, Los Angeles, Calif.

Circus Girl. 14 x 8. Collection Mr. and Mrs. Joseph Resnick, Ellenville, N.Y.

Scholar. 10 x 8. Collection Mr. and Mrs. Chester Sennet, Great Neck, N.Y.

Before the Party. 14 x 18. Collection Mr. and Mrs. Joseph W. Finver, West Hempstead, N.Y.

Seated Figure. 30 x 38. Collection Mr. and Mrs. Michael Halperin, New York.

Lagin Family. 30 x 24. Collection Mr. and Mrs. Nathan Lagin, Great Neck, N.Y.

Pearl. 20 x 16. Collection Mr. and Mrs. Bruno Weinschel, Bethesda, Md.

Figure. 34 x 28. Collection Mr. and Mrs. Irving L. Korn, Great Neck, N.Y.

Woman. 34 x 28. Collection Mr. and Mrs. Abraham Frankel, Cedarhurst, N.Y.

Prof. Norman Schell. 26 x 18. Massachusetts Institute of Technology, Cambridge, Mass.

Woman in Blue. 37 x 27. Collection Mrs. Selma Raifman, Brooklyn, N.Y.

Amiel Children. 30 x 24. Collection Jack Amiel, New York.

1954   Reclining Figure. 29 x 35. Collection Mr. and Mrs. Martin Gabel, New York.

Brian and Judy. 14 x 11. Collection Mr. and Mrs. Alex E. Genson, East Rockaway, N.Y.

Girl Reading. 10 x 8. Collection Mr. and Mrs. Cyrus Brin, New York.

The Actor. 13 x 7. Collection Mr. and Mrs. Arthur Golden, Kings Point, N.Y.

Harbor. 18 x 32. Collection Mr. and Mrs. Harry Horowitz, Great Neck, N.Y.

Pamela Mia. 24 x 18. Collection Mr. and Mrs. Charles F. Paul, Oyster Bay, N.Y.

Dorothy. 32 x 26. Collection Mr. and Mrs. Jerome Klein, New York.

Boats. 20 x 8. Collection Mr. and Mrs. Harold P. Heller, Bayside, N.Y.

Ina. 40 x 30. Collection Mr. and Mrs. Calvin Bell, Kings Point, N.Y.

Two Girls. 17 x 13. Collection Mr. and Mrs. Reuben L. Kershaw, Great Neck, N.Y. (Pl. 31)

Leslie. 12 x 15. Collection Dr. and Mrs. Martin Langsam, Brooklyn, N.Y.

Reclining Figure. 4 x 6. Collection Mr. and Mrs. Abe Burrows, New York.

Figures. 24 x 20. Collection Mr. and Mrs. Samuel Diamond, Brooklyn, N.Y.

Prayer. 26 x 12. Collection Mr. and Mrs. Robert H. Avnet, Los Angeles, Calif.

Rabbi. 18 x 11. Collection Mr. and Mrs. Stanford Schwartzman, Englewood Cliffs, N.J.

Dressing. 13 x 22. Collection Dr. and Mrs. Eugene Saland, Old Westbury, N.Y. (Pl. 32)

Reading. 32 x 14. Collection Mr. and Mrs. Al Schwartz, Kings Point, N.Y.

Dancer. 12 x 10. Collection Judge and Mrs. Harold Tessler, Jamaica Estates, N.Y.

Primping. 26 x 16. Collection Mr. and Mrs. Burton R. Sims, Roslyn, N.Y.

Girl on Chair. 10 x 8. Collection Gladys Filmus. (Pl. 37)

At the Museum. 30 x 16. ACA Gallery, New York. (Pl. 33)

The Red Sweater. 14 x 11. Collection Gladys Filmus. (Pl. 30)

Norcey. 24 x 20. Collection Dr. Harry Katz, New York.

Rabbi Joseph Miller. 30 x 24. Congregation Shaare Torah, Brooklyn, N.Y.

Seated Figure. 30 x 24. Collection Mr. and Mrs. Samuel Rosenthal, Brooklyn, N.Y.

Acrobats. 18 x 40. Collection Mr. and Mrs. Jack Nodiff, East Rockaway, N.Y.

Father. 20 x 16. Collection Mr. and Mrs. Leon Jolson, Kings Point, N.Y.

1955   Ballet. 22 x 18. Collection Mr. and Mrs. Maurice L. Broder, Roslyn, N.Y.
Exhibit. 11 x 14. Collection Mr. and Mrs. Benjamin Ganeles, Mount Vernon, N.Y.
Mother and Child. 14 x 8. Collection Mr. and Mrs. Arthur Golden, Kings Point, N.Y.
At the Exhibition. 8 x 10. Collection Mr. and Mrs. Harry Kerr, Cedarhurst, N.Y.
Ben. 20 x 16. Collection Mr. and Mrs. Ben Koehl, Kings Point, N.Y.
Scholar. 8 x 10. Collection Mr. and Mrs. Raymond Kay, Great Neck, N.Y.
Children. 37 x 43. Collection Mr. and Mrs. Arthur E. Jacobs, Lynbrook, N.Y.
Sisters. 24 x 22. Collection Mr. and Mrs. Meyer Epstein, Jamaica Estates, N.Y.
Artist and Model. 30 x 24. Collection Mr. and Mrs. Robert H. Avnet, Los Angeles, Calif.
Music Makers. 20 x 26. Collection Mr. and Mrs. Arnold Rosenberg, Great Neck, N.Y. (Pl. 35)
April. 14 x 30. Collection Mr. and Mrs. Joseph Resnick, Ellenville, N.Y. (Pl. 39)
Musicians. 20 x 16. Collection Mrs. Gail Turner, Great Neck, N.Y.
Mother and Child. 24 x 18. Collection Dr. and Mrs. Jack Topal, Flushing, N.Y.
Portrait of Dr. Harry Katz. 24 x 20. Collection Dr. Harry Katz, New York.
Rubin Children. 14 x 11. Collection Mr. and Mrs. Seymour Rubin, Roslyn, N.Y.
Umbrellas. 13 x 21. Collection Mrs. Sydel Atlas, New York.
Young Girl. 20 x 16. Collection Mr. and Mrs. Louis M. Wolf, Great Neck, N.Y.
Lyle. 22 x 18. Collection Mr. and Mrs. David Gumer, Great Neck, N.Y.
Louisa and David. 30 x 24. Collection Mr. and Mrs. David Gumer, Great Neck, N.Y.
Figures with Flowers. 30 x 24. Collection Mr. and Mrs. Max Brecker, Jamaica Estates, N.Y.
Elaine and Alan. 20 x 16. Collection Mr. and Mrs. David Gumer, Great Neck, N.Y.
Laura. 30 x 24. Collection Dr. and Mrs. Ralph Wogalter, Richmond, Va.
Portrait of Mrs. Thomas E. Dewey. 32 x 26. Collection former Governor and
    Mrs. Thomas E. Dewey, New York.
Rebecca. 24 x 20. Collection Mrs. Selma Raifman, Brooklyn, N.Y.

1956   Rehearsal Break. 14 x 11. Collection Mr. and Mrs. Sam Aronowitz, Great Neck, N.Y.
Young Woman. 16 x 12. Collection Mr. and Mrs. Theodore Bergman, Great Neck, N.Y.
The Flute Player. 11 x 14. Collection Dr. and Mrs. Arthur S. Carlson, Glen Cove, N.Y. (Pl. 34)
At the Window. 30 x 18. Collection Mr. and Mrs. Abner Diamond, Brooklyn, N.Y.
In the Rain. 16 x 30. Collection Mr. and Mrs. Richard Bergman, Kings Point, N.Y.
Alice and Zack. 22 x 16. Collection Mr. and Mrs. Murray Brauer, Kings Point, N.Y.
Terry. 24 x 20. Collection Mr. and Mrs. George Hillman, East Meadow, N.Y.
Nora. 34 x 23. ACA Gallery, New York.
Dancers. 18 x 44. Collection Mr. and Mrs. Jack Clareman, Great Neck, N.Y.
Robin and Madelyn. 25 x 21. Collection Mr. and Mrs. Calvin Bell, Kings Point, N.Y.
Fisherman. 32 x 14. Collection Dr. and Mrs. Alexander Levine, Brooklyn, N.Y.
At the Museum. 26 x 14. Collection Dr. and Mrs. Alexander Levine, Brooklyn, N.Y.
Valerie. 16 x 12. Collection Mr. and Mrs. Jules Milton, Great Neck, N.Y.
Exhibition. 30 x 16. Collection Mr. and Mrs. Samuel Dorsky, Kings Point, N.Y.
The Teacher. 16 x 10. Collection Mr. and Mrs. Lawrence Posner, Brooklyn, N.Y.
Young Couple. 30 x 16. Collection Mr. and Mrs. Bernard Jacobson, Great Neck, N.Y.
Children. 14 x 11. Collection Mr. and Mrs. Leonard Milton, Great Neck, N.Y.
Sailing. 27 x 26. Collection Mr. and Mrs. Leonard Milton, Great Neck, N.Y.
Grandparents. 20 x 16. Collection Mr. and Mrs. Leonard Milton, Great Neck, N.Y.
Woman in White. 39 x 30. Collection Mr. and Mrs. Leonard Milton, Great Neck, N.Y.
Kathy. 20 x 16. Collection Mr. and Mrs. Theodore Wilentz, New York.
Still Life. 24 x 40. Collection Mr. and Mrs. William Wolf, Hewlitt Harbor, N.Y.
Figure. 30 x 36. Collection Mr. and Mrs. William Wolf, Hewlitt Harbor, N.Y.
Milan. 14 x 11. Collection Mr. and Mrs. Ben Segall, Brooklyn, N.Y.
Rain. 22 x 12. Collection Dr. and Mrs. Sidney Samis, Kings Point, N.Y. (Pl. 40)
Sisters. 14 x 11. Collection Mr. and Mrs. Arthur Tucker, Merrick, N.Y.
Gallery. 9 x 12. Collection Mr. and Mrs. Benjamin Waldbaum, Cedarhurst, N.Y.
Sewing. 10 x 8. Collection Dr. and Mrs. Jack Topal, Flushing, N.Y.

Exhibit. 23 x 19. Collection Dr. and Mrs. Jack Topal, Flushing, N.Y.

Denise and Iris. 14 x 11. Collection Mr. and Mrs. Aaron Rubin, New Hyde Park, N.Y.

Rabbi Jacob P. Rudin. 42 x 34. Temple Beth-El, Great Neck, N.Y.

Betty. 10 x 8. Collection Mr. and Mrs. Samuel Friedland, Brooklyn, N.Y.

Two Dancers. 16 x 20. Collection Mr. and Mrs. Bruno Lucchesi, New York.

Grandmother. 20 x 16. Collection Mrs. Anna Rubin, Bayside, N.Y.

Children. 14 x 11. Collection Mr. and Mrs. Abe Rubin, New York.

Scholar. 10 x 9. Collection Mr. and Mrs. Mark Mason, New York.

Woman in White. 30 x 24. Collection Mr. and Mrs. Misha Davidson, Roslyn, N.Y.

The Children. 14 x 11. Collection Mr. and Mrs. Misha Davidson, Roslyn, N.Y.

Gossips. 16 x 20. ACA Gallery, New York. (Pl. 36)

1957 The Student. 24 x 30. Collection Mr. and Mrs. Benjamin Alpert, Kings Point, N.Y.

Clown. 14 x 11. Collection Jonathan Avnet, Kings Point, N.Y. (Pl. 49)

Girl. 24 x 14. Collection Mr. and Mrs. Edward Bauman, Great Neck, N.Y.

Bacchanal. 48 x 44. Collection Mr. and Mrs. Lester Avnet, Kings Point, N.Y.

Exhibition. 10 x 12. Collection Mr. and Mrs. Fred Einsidler, Great Neck, N.Y.

Procession. 34 x 12. Collection Mr. and Mrs. Herman Gross, Great Neck, N.Y.

Sunday in the Museum. 16 x 30. Collection Mr. and Mrs. Arthur P. Gould, Great Neck, N.Y. (Pl. 42)

Fisherman. 14 x 30. Collection Mr. and Mrs. Harry Horowitz, Great Neck, N.Y.

Still Life. 60 x 47. Collection Mr. and Mrs. Lester Avnet, Kings Point, N.Y.

Seated Figure. 32 x 26. Collection Mr. and Mrs. Sidney Jacobson, Great Neck, N.Y.

In the Garden. 30 x 24. Collection Mr. and Mrs. Everett Barel, West Hempstead, N.Y.

Exhibition Opening. 20 x 26. Collection Dr. and Mrs. Norman Avnet, Great Neck, N.Y. (Pl. 41)

Children. 14 x 11. Collection Mr. and Mrs. Sidney Jacobson, Great Neck, N.Y.

Ballerinas. 18 x 44. Collection Mr. and Mrs. Sidney Jacobson, Great Neck, N.Y.

Esther. 32 x 26. Collection Mr. and Mrs. Seymour S. Kane, Manhattan Beach, N.Y.

Gallery. 16 x 10. Collection Mr. and Mrs. Joseph Resnick, Ellenville, N.Y.

Girl Reading. 14 x 11. ACA Gallery, New York. (Pl. 38)

Exhibition. 16 x 9. Collection Mr. and Mrs. Mark Mason, New York.

Embrace. 14 x 11. Collection Mr. and Mrs. Bernard Jacobson, Great Neck, N.Y.

Barbara. 32 x 26. Collection Mr. and Mrs. Irving J. Rivkin, Brooklyn, N.Y.

Figure in the Garden. 34 x 28. Collection Mr. and Mrs. Melvin Kass, New Hyde Park, N.Y.

Woman with a Cat. 32 x 16. Collection Mr. and Mrs. Joseph Resnick, Ellenville, N.Y.

Three Girls. 10 x 8. Collection Mr. and Mrs. Al Schwartz, Kings Point, N.Y. (Pl. 44)

Rubin Children. 14 x 11. Collection Mr. and Mrs. Matthew Rubin, Bellrose, N.Y.

Adolescence. 32 x 28. Collection Mrs. Harry Shapiro, Jamaica, N.Y.

Grandchildren. 24 x 36. Collection Mr. and Mrs. Nat A. Barell, Brooklyn, N.Y.

The Flowered Hat. 32 x 26. Collection Mr. and Mrs. Bernard Wexler, Great Neck, N.Y.

Kleinman Children. 14 x 11. Collection Mr. and Mrs. Seymour Kleinman, Great Neck, N.Y.

1958 Sunday Afternoon. 12 x 22. Collection Mr. and Mrs. Benjamin Alpert, Kings Point, N.Y.

Girl in Blue. 30 x 14. Collection Charles Avnet, Long Beach, N.Y. (Pl. 43)

Flute Player. 11 x 14. Collection Dr. and Mrs. Abraham Berens, Brooklyn, N.Y.

Farmer and Wife. 34 x 19. Collection Mr. and Mrs. Theodore Bergman, Great Neck, N.Y.

Exhibit. 18 x 14. Collection Mr. and Mrs. Sidney Berg, Kings Point, N.Y.

Violinist. 18 x 8. Collection Mr. and Mrs. Martin C. Barell, Kings Point, N.Y.

At the Gallery. 16 x 20. Collection Mr. and Mrs. Seymour Kleinman, Great Neck, N.Y. (Pl. 45)

Backstage. 30 x 40. Collection Mr. and Mrs. Lester Avnet, Kings Point, N.Y. (Pl. 56)

Procession. 38 x 11. Collection Mr. and Mrs. Louis Feldman, Woodmere, N.Y.

Trees. 26 x 20. Collection Mr. and Mrs. Stanford Schwartzman, Englewood Cliffs, N.J.

The Bridge. 40 x 49. Collection Mr. and Mrs. Ian Starr, Wantagh, N.Y.

Judy. 10 x 8. Collection Dr. and Mrs. Jack Rosen, Brooklyn, N.Y.

Portrait of Dr. Abraham Rabiner. 36 x 30. Kings County Hospital, Brooklyn, N.Y.

Portrait of Dr. Julius Dobkin. 14 x 11. Collection Mrs. Rose Dobkin, Bronx, N.Y.

David and Ella. 14 x 11. Collection Mrs. Rose Dobkin, Bronx, N.Y.

Girl at the Window. 30 x 20. ACA Gallery, New York.

Rose. 14 x 11. Collection Mrs. Rose Dobkin, Bronx, N.Y.

Dress Rehearsal. 16 x 12. Collection Mr. and Mrs. Jack Nodiff, East Rockaway, N.Y.

Portrait of Sidney. 20 x 16. Collection Mr. and Mrs. Sidney Kotimsky, New York.

Lonely Horse. 18 x 22. Collection Dr. and Mrs. Benjamin Schultz, Great Neck, N.Y.

Birds. 30 x 36. Collection Mr. and Mrs. Harry Ashley, Great Neck, N.Y.

Schultz Family. 14 x 11. Collection Dr. and Mrs. Benjamin Schultz, Great Neck, N.Y.

Summer Rain. 13 x 24. Collection Mr. and Mrs. Martin C. Barell, Kings Point, N.Y. (Pl. 48)

Nora. 34 x 23. ACA Gallery, New York. (Pl. 46)

The Hora. 34 x 23. Collection Dr. and Mrs. Jack Rosen, Brooklyn, N.Y. (Pl. 58)

1959   Reading Room. 20 x 30. ACA Gallery, New York. (Pl. 59)

Girl with Braid. 30 x 14. Collection Charles Avnet, Long Beach, N.Y.

Two Dancers. 16 x 12. Collection Mr. and Mrs. Joseph Resnick, Ellenville, N.Y. (Pl. 10)

Portrait of Ben. 30 x 24. Collection Mr. and Mrs. Benjamin Alpert, Kings Point, N.Y.

Conversation. 30 x 24. Collection Mr. and Mrs. Harry Cooper, Brooklyn, N.Y.

Grandfather. 18 x 28. Collection Mr. and Mrs. Arthur P. Gould, Great Neck, N.Y.

Portrait of Dr. Alexander Levine. 30 x 24. Collection Dr. and Mrs. Alexander Levine, Brooklyn, N.Y.

Children. 14 x 11. Collection Dr. and Mrs. Alexander Levine, Brooklyn, N.Y.

Woman on Balcony. 30 x 16. Collection Mr. and Mrs. Sam Marks, Burbank, Calif. (Pl. 53)

Lydia. 30 x 24. Collection Dr. and Mrs. Alexander Levine, Brooklyn, N.Y.

Stooped Old Man. 24 x 14. ACA Gallery, New York. (Pl. 47)

Harlequin. 50 x 26. Collection Mr. and Mrs. Oscar Reiss, Kings Point, N.Y.

Youth. 30 x 24. Collection Mr. and Mrs. Sol Uman, Freeport, N.Y.

Lisa. 34 x 20. Collection Mr. and Mrs. Lester Avnet, Kings Point, N.Y. (Pl. 51)

Discussion. 26 x 16. Collection Mr. and Mrs. Charles Schnell, Maplewood, N.J.

Nude. 34 x 12. ACA Gallery, New York. (Pl. 60)

Musicians. 30 x 40. Collection Charles Avnet, Long Beach, N.Y.

Nora. 30 x 20. Collection Mr. and Mrs. Joseph Edelstein, Kings Point, N.Y.

Pretzel Vendor. 14 x 11. Collection Chaim Shursha, Tel-Aviv, Israel. (Pl. 52)

After Work. 26 x 10. ACA Gallery, New York. (Pl. 61)

1960   At the Exhibition. 30 x 24. Collection Mr. and Mrs. Moe Goldberg, Brooklyn, N.Y.

Ballerina. 34 x 20. Collection Mr. and Mrs. David Grayson, Roslyn, N.Y.

Quintet. 16 x 20. Collection Mr. and Mrs. Seymour Kleinman, Great Neck, N.Y.

Blue Jeans. 34 x 20. Collection Mr. and Mrs. David Grayson, Roslyn, New York.

Paul. 34 x 20. Collection Mr. and Mrs. David Grayson, Roslyn, N.Y.

Figure. 50 x 26. Collection Dr. and Mrs. Karl Neimand, Great Neck, N.Y.

The Children. 14 x 11. Collection Dr. and Mrs. Karl Neimand, Great Neck, N.Y.

Seated Figure. 25 x 20. Collection Mr. and Mrs. Laurence W. Licht, Great Neck, N.Y.

Old Friends. 20 x 14. Collection Mr. and Mrs. Boris M. Tarna, Tokyo, Japan. (Pl. 62)

Joyce and Jaynee. 14 x 11. Collection Mr. and Mrs. Laurence L. Licht, Great Neck, N.Y.

Talmudic Student. 20 x 26. Collection Mr. and Mrs. Lester Avnet, Kings Point, N.Y.

Lovers. 42 x 32. Collection Mr. and Mrs. Lewis Dean Katz, New York.

Two Figures. 30 x 24. Collection Mr. and Mrs. Hyman B. Mack, Jamaica Estates, N.Y.

Tevya. 26 x 10. Collection Mr. and Mrs. Robert Forest, Rockville Center, N.Y.

Zemach. 30 x 20. Collection Dr. and Mrs. Norman Avnet, Great Neck, N.Y.

Grandfather. 20 x 16. Collection Dr. and Mrs. Norman Avnet, Great Neck, N.Y.

Bible Study. 16 x 20. ACA Gallery, New York.

Man with a Flute. 12 x 15. Collection Mr. and Mrs. George Rich, Glen Cove, N.Y.

The Shy One. 26 x 10. Collection Mr. and Mrs. George Rich, Glen Cove, N.Y.

Benjamin Zemach. 30 x 16. Collection Mr. and Mrs. Robert H. Avnet, Los Angeles, Calif.

Ruth. 30 x 24. Collection Mr. and Mrs. Joseph Resnick, Ellenville, N.Y.

Young Boy. 12 x 14. Collection Mr. and Mrs. Irving Winston, Woodmere, N.Y.

Figure. 18 x 14. Collection Mr. and Mrs. Irving Winston, Woodmere, N.Y.

Woman. 18 x 14. Collection Mr. and Mrs. Irving Winston, Woodmere, N.Y.

Portrait of Frank Kleinholz. 16 x 12. Collection Mr. and Mrs. Frank Kleinholz, Port Washington, N.Y.

Dressing Room. 26 x 36. Collection Mr. and Mrs. Lester Avnet, Kings Point. N.Y. (Pl. 57)

Portrait of Elsie Rudin. 24 x 20. Temple Beth-El, Great Neck, N.Y.

Woman in Blue. 50 x 28. Collection Mr. and Mrs. Martin C. Barell, Kings Point, N.Y.

Seated Figure. 24 x 20. Collection Mr. and Mrs. Bertram Hollander, New York.

The Merinoff Children. 60 x 66. Collection Herman Merinoff, Great Neck, N.Y.

The Painter. 16 x 12. Collection Mr. and Mrs. Samuel L. Shore, Kings Point, N.Y.

Artist's Wife. 24 x 14. Collection of the artist. (Pl. 50)

Giovanna. 14 x 11. ACA Gallery, New York. (Pl. 54)

Morning Paper. 24 x 14. ACA Gallery, .New York. (Pl. 63)

1961   Chassidic Dance. 36 x 28. Collection Dr. and Mrs. Norman Avnet, Great Neck, N.Y. (Pl. 65)

Seated Figure. 30 x 24. Collection Mr. and Mrs. Alfred Grien, Kings Point, N.Y.

Rejoicing. 23 x 18. Collection Mr. and Mrs. Seymour Kleinman, Great Neck, N.Y.

Patriarch. 26 x 10. Collection Dr. and Mrs. Norman Avnet, Great Neck, N.Y. (Pl. 67)

Debby and Karen. 14 x 11. Collection Mr. and Mrs. Norton Zavon, Great Neck, N.Y.

Uncle Tevya. 26 x 12. Collection Mr. and Mrs. George Holland, Brooklyn, N.Y.

Kate. 22 x 18. Collection Mr. and Mrs. Oscar Abrin, Ormond Beach, Fla.

Wachtel Children. 14 x 11. Collection Mr. and Mrs. Harry Wachtel, Kings Point, N.Y.

Stephen. 20 x 14. Collection Stephen Isaac Filmus. (Pl. 69)

The Concert. 30 x 40. Collection Mr. and Mrs. Robert H. Avnet, Los Angeles, Calif. (Pl. 79)

Connoisseur. 13 x 6. Collection of the artist. (Pl. 78)

The Klezmer. 26 x 32. Collection Mr. and Mrs. Lester Avnet, Kings Point, N.Y. (Pl. 74)

Point of Information. 16 x 30. ACA Gallery, New York. (Pl. 66)

Festivities. 30 x 40. Collection Mr. and Mrs. Joseph Edelstein, Kings Point, N.Y.

The Shy One. 17 x 10. Collection Miss Dale Kleinman, Great Neck, N.Y.

The Wedding Dance. 24 x 44. Collection Dr. and Mrs. Alexander Levine, Brooklyn, N.Y.

Ruth and Paul. 35 x 26. Collection Mr. and Mrs. Paul Faske, North Miami, Fla.

1962   Portrait of Lester Avnet. 36 x 30. Collection Mr. and Mrs. Lester Avnet, Kings Point, N.Y.

Michael. 20 x 14. Collection Michael Roy Filmus. (Pl. 68)

The Discussion. 29 x 14. Collection Dr. and Mrs. Norman Avnet, Great Neck, N.Y. (Pl. 64)

Fiddler. 26 x 12. Collection Dr. and Mrs. Norman Avnet, Great Neck, N.Y.

Man Reading. 26 x 20. Collection Mr. and Mrs. Paul Faske, North Miami, Fla.

The Wedding. 24 x 44. Collection Mr. and Mrs. Paul Faske, North Miami, Fla.

Elaine. 36 x 30. Collection Herman Merinoff, Great Neck, N.Y.

Preserving the Torah. 23 x 34. ACA Gallery, New York. (Pl. 71)

Conversation. 30 x 24. Collection Mr. and Mrs. Paul Faske, North Miami, Fla.

Center Lake. 32 x 26. Collection Mr. and Mrs. Sheldon Hoch, Mount Vernon, N.Y.

Trio. 30 x 40. ACA Gallery, New York. (Pl. 73)

Sextet. 36 x 26. ACA Gallery, New York.

Print Collector. 24 x 20. Collection Dr. and Mrs. Theodore Robertson, Locust Valley, N.Y. (Pl. 77)

The Orchestra. 30 x 40. Collection Mr. and Mrs. Lester Avnet, Kings Point, N.Y. (Pl. 75)

The Return. 26 x 12. ACA Gallery, New York. (Pl. 70)

Art Experts. 14 x 28. ACA Gallery, New York.

At the Piano. 14 x 19. Collection Mr. and Mrs. Lester Avnet, Kings Point, N.Y. (Pl. 76)

Chamber Music. 36 x 26. ACA Gallery, New York. (Pl. 72)

1963   Jugglers. 30 x 36. Collection Mr. and Mrs. Everett Barel, West Hempstead, N.Y.

Stanley Jay. 30 x 24. Collection Mr. and Mrs. Marvin Ross, Manhasset Hills, N.Y.

Old Scholar. 10 x 8. Collection of the artist. (Pl. 81)

Self-Portrait. 20 x 26. Collection of the artist. (Pl. 3)

Circus Girl. 30 x 20. ACA Gallery, New York. (Pl. 55)

The Village. 30 x 50. ACA Gallery, New York. (Pl. 80)